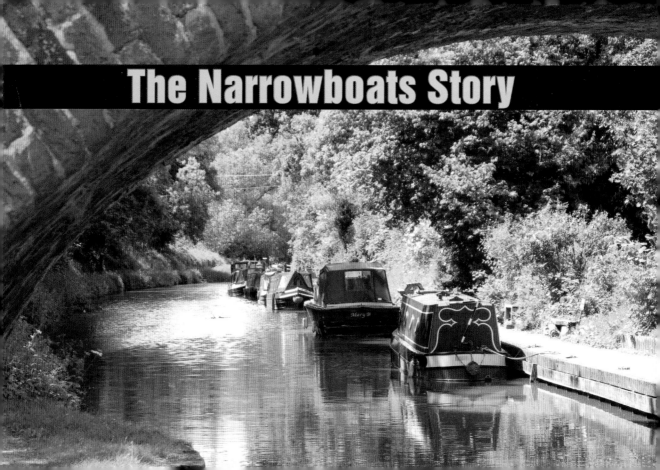

The Narrowboats Story

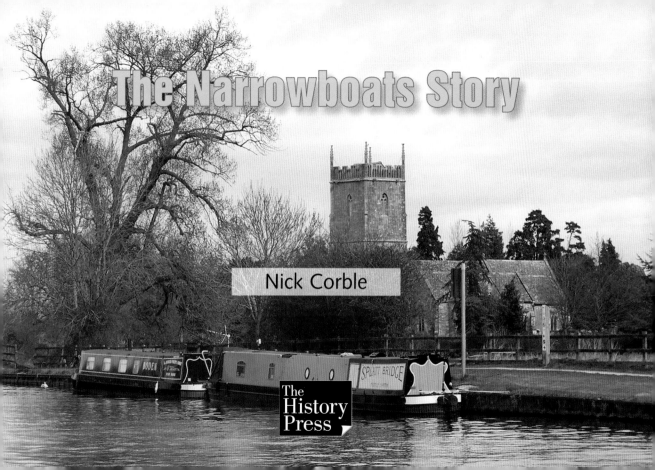

The Narrowboats Story

Nick Corble

The History Press

Published in the United Kingdom in 2012 by
The History Press
The Mill · Brimscombe Port · Stroud · Gloucestershire · GL5 2QG

British Library Cataloguing in Publication Data
A catalogue record for this book is available from the British
Library.

Hardback ISBN 978-0-7524-6482-4

Half title page:
Who's around the corner?

Title page:
*A quiet morning on the
Gloucester & Sharpness
Canal. (Courtesy of E.
Locke)*

➤ *Owners still like to
add a splash of colour to
their boats. (Courtesy of
Allan Ford)*

Typesetting and origination by The History Press
Manufacturing managed by Jellyfish Print Solutions Ltd
Printed in India

CONTENTS

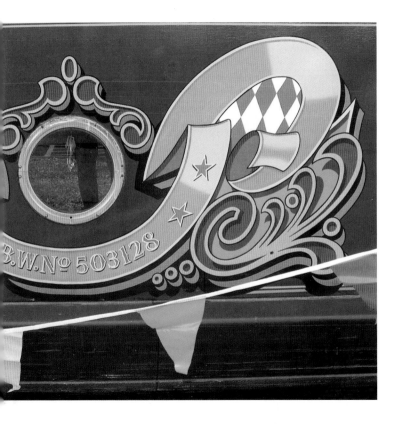

ACKNOWLEDGEMENTS

A number of different people and organisations have been helpful in preparing this book and I would like to thank them for their contributions. Particular gratitude goes out to Allan Ford and to British Waterways for their help in sourcing illustrations. Others to whom a debt is owed include Andrew Denny, Blisworth Images, Dudley Archives, The Horse Boating Society, Manchester City Library, Salford City Council and Warrington Museum and Art Gallery.

Where attribution is possible it has been given, otherwise the photographs in this book tend to be taken by myself, although in some cases, as with postcards, it has not been possible to discover to whom credit should be given.

In 1746 the Young Pretender was defeated at Culloden, putting the final seal on the Act of Union with Scotland agreed just under forty years previously. At last the country could call itself a truly United Kingdom.

Although this may have been true politically, the reality on the ground was very different. A demographic map of the country would have looked like a random ink splat, with one big dot representing London and hundreds of much smaller dots representing the other towns and villages around it. Most local market towns had residents numbering in the thousands at best, whilst London outnumbered its nearest rivals by a factor of at least ten.

Furthermore, moving around this 'united kingdom' was something attempted only by the rich, the desperate or the brave.

The only viable alternative to walking was to travel by horse or stagecoach, a privilege accorded to just a few. Roads, although improving with the introduction of turnpikes (an early form of toll road), were simply dangerous. Kept in poor repair and open to the vagaries of the weather, if the mud didn't get you the vermin or

▼ *By the mid-eighteenth century London was a large metropolis.*

criminals that lined them probably would. Little wonder that very few Britons ever wandered further than their neighbouring parish.

Yet signs of change were beginning to appear. Pockets of local industry were forming and qualities we would label today as 'entrepreneurialism' were taking hold. By 1776 the economist Adam Smith would be lauding the idea of a high-production, high-wage economy based on economies of scale in large factories in his seminal work *The Wealth of Nations*.

At the same time, the potential of the generous abundance of natural mineral resources the country had been blessed with was just beginning to be tapped. Coal in particular was being used to heat homes and fire industrial processes and the steam age was just around the corner. On top of all this the sheer number of people in the country was growing fast.

There was a problem, however. Economic power remained heavily skewed towards London, and it was proving increasingly difficult to physically provide enough food and consumer goods to satisfy this massive market. The larger provincial towns were facing similar problems, limiting their potential to provide an economic counterweight. Transporting anything that

▼ *Manchester meanwhile remained little more than a small town.*

couldn't fit on the back of a cart, man or donkey represented a significant logistical challenge. Where there were rivers goods could be transported by boat, but rivers didn't always obey the wishes of men, both in terms of where they flowed and how they flowed.

Nowhere were these problems better illustrated than in Manchester. A population of 10,000 at the start of the eighteenth century soared to nearer 70,000 by the end, making the town the second largest centre in the country. The town was becoming a manufacturing hub for cotton, linen and silk, but feeding both the people and the demands of industry had become increasingly difficult. Bad weather, something not uncommon in Manchester, would waterlog the roads, effectively giving the town all the characteristics of being

under siege for months at a time. Food riots were common, not least because the land around the town was too poor to grow anything of value, and there were no forests for wood. That same land, however, was abundant in the other commodity the town depended upon:

Stagecoaches were for the rich, and even then were high risk.

9

➤ Horsepower was much more effective when used pulling a boat.

Did you know?
In the 1750s three stagecoaches a week plied the route between London and Manchester, taking four days to get there. Passengers were advised that the service only ran 'God Willing'.

A rare example of a turf-sided lock, at Monkey Marsh on the Kennet and Avon Canal.

Did you know?
Having increased by only a million during the seventeenth century, the population of the UK grew by 3 million in the following hundred years, reaching 8 million.

coal. As with the food, the difficulty was finding a way of transporting it.

Luckily, one man was determined to solve the problem. Equally fortuitously, he chanced upon another man who had the skills to help him do so and a third who made sure the other two men's plans became a reality. Combined, the vision and perseverance of these three men were to show not just Manchester, but the whole country, how to move bulk goods efficiently and cheaply over long distances. In so doing, these three men were to provide the spark that was to ignite the Industrial Revolution.

Using water to transport heavy goods wasn't anything new. The problem was that rivers could be mercurial, flowing where they wanted, often subject to tides, hidden rocks and weirs – features which made using them a dangerous business.

Efforts had been made to make rivers easier to negotiate. By 1660 there were 680 miles of navigable river in the UK, and over the next seventy-five years improvements to the Aire in Yorkshire and the Avon, Kennet and Wey in the south added a further 500 miles to this total. These improved rivers became known as 'navigations', a term still in use today, but they remained human adjustments to natural phenomena, and as such each was at best a compromise.

Equally, the notion of totally artificial waterways, independent of rivers, whose flows could be controlled by men, wasn't a new one and, as with so many other things, the Romans had led the way. As with plumbing and road building these useful skills had been lost, however, and

▼ *The newer Barton Aqueduct across the Manchester Ship Canal is still a waterways marvel, in that it can swing.*

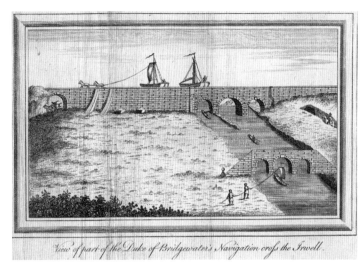
View of part of the Duke of Bridgewater's Navigation cross the Irwell.

▲ *How Brindley's Barton Aqueduct would have looked – note the sails on the boats. (Courtesy of Frank Mullineux Collection, Salford City Council)*

was the first in Britain to use 'pound' locks: chambers secured by wooden gates in which boats could rise or fall through the controlled release or addition of water, with the sides of the lock covered in turf. Ingenious though this was, the idea didn't catch on and it took another hundred years before the idea of locks was used again, as part of the improvements to the Wey. While canals on a grand scale took off in France, with the Canal du Midi opening in 1681, the notion was slow to catch on across the Channel.

The next attempt to create a totally independent canal had to wait for a further seventy-five years, until 1737, when Scroop Egerton, the First Duke of Bridgewater, applied to Parliament for an Act to convert a brook linking his coal mines at Worsley west of Manchester to

Britain had to wait over a thousand years before attempts were made to revive canal-building, and even this was brief.

Opened in 1566, the Exeter Canal was a five-mile waterway built to by-pass a particularly troublesome weir. This canal

Brindley's Aqueduct just before it was demolished. (Courtesy of Frank Mullineux Collection, Salford City Council)

Did you know?
A horse can pull sixty times more weight than it can carry.

Monument to the Third Duke of Bridgewater on his estate in Ashridge, which refers to him as 'The Father of Inland Navigation'.

that growing town. In the end the idea came to nought, defeated on the grounds of both practicality and cost, as well as opposition from vested interests, notably the existing Mersey and Irwell Navigation and the owners of turnpike roads.

It took another twenty years for a canal to be actually cut, this time by the Corporation of Liverpool rather than a duke. Initially viewed as a navigational improvement to the Sankey Brook, linking the Mersey about two miles below Warrington to St Helens, the brook didn't really qualify as a river and in time the cut became recognised formally as the St Helens Canal.

At this point our story returns to Worsley and the Egerton family. The first Duke of Bridgewater had died in 1744, having squired eight children, including four sons. The oldest of these had died aged only six, while the third only just made it past his first birthday. On Scroop's death the title passed to his second son, John, who was only seventeen at the time. The final son, Francis, who was nine, quickly became forgotten as his mother remarried, and he ended up passing through the hands of a succession of tutors. Not seen as particularly promising, and sickly to boot, few saw the value in over-educating the boy.

It came as something of a shock to all concerned therefore when John Egerton died four years later, leaving Francis to become the third Duke at the tender age of twelve. Plans were rapidly put into place to regain lost time. Francis was given two aristocratic guardians and five years later he was sent on a Grand Tour of Europe. Here he was captivated more by triumphs of engineering than of art, and it is perfectly possible that he saw the Canal du Midi in France along the way.

On returning to England he adopted the life of a playboy, indulging himself in horseracing (both as a punter and a

James Brindley, with his trademark surveying instrument. (Courtesy of Frank Mullineux Collection, Salford City Council)

Did you know?
The Romans had dug waterways in the Fens, initially as drainage channels but also providing a means of transporting grain between garrisons.

► The Calder and Hebble Navigation today; note how much wider it is than a traditional canal.

participant) and affairs of the heart. It was one such affair that was to change his life. Rebutted in love, Francis eventually retreated to one of his estates, that at Worsley in Cheshire, far away from London society. It was here, along with his agent John Gilbert, that he became intrigued by his father's idea of an artificial waterway to transport coal to Manchester.

Initially apprenticed at Boultons of Birmingham, later to become pioneers in steam, John Gilbert had been recommended to Francis Egerton, and the two quickly formed a strong working bond. Both were intrigued by the possibility of retrieving coal from the Duke's mines and transporting it to Manchester, but as well as the logistical and political problems experienced twenty years before there was also the matter of the constant flooding in the mines.

Ford Madox Brown's Mural in Manchester Town Hall, with a fanciful representation of the opening of the Barton Aqueduct.

It was at this point that a third man entered the frame, forming what was to become known as 'the triumvirate', a combination of personalities, perseverance and ingenuity that was to bring about the country's first true canal. That third man was James Brindley, born in Derbyshire of humble stock, who nevertheless from an early age showed what was later to be called a 'particular facility with water'.

remained. Brindley took these up with relish, leaving the Duke to manage the political side of things, not least gaining the necessary parliamentary approval. Undoubtedly the most significant of these problems was crossing the River Irwell. As in his father's time, the Mersey and Irwell

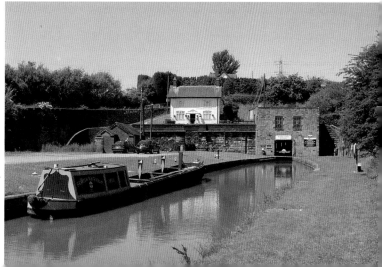

Following an apprenticeship as a millwright, during which he'd shown promise as an engineer, Brindley had forged a reputation as someone capable of resolving the problem of flooding mines.

It seems that the idea of using water drained from the mines to feed an artificial waterway pre-dated Brindley, but those troublesome logistical problems had

A plan of the route of the Trent and Mersey Canal. (Courtesy of British Waterways)

The Packet House at Worsley, where modern canals began.

Navigation was a powerful force, to whom the idea of a canal represented a potentially serious competitor.

In order to reach Manchester the proposed canal would have to lower itself, craft would then have to cross over the river and be raised up again. The Navigation, seeing its chance, played its ace and proposed ruinous charges to allow canal craft to cross their waterway. They hadn't reckoned on James Brindley.

Brindley's solution was to go over the Irwell with an aqueduct at Barton, an engineering feat unparalleled since Roman times in Britain. Called 'the waterway in the sky', most predicted it was impossible and the opening day was packed with crowds anticipating a spectacular failure. They were to be disappointed. Instead, what they witnessed was a triumph, both

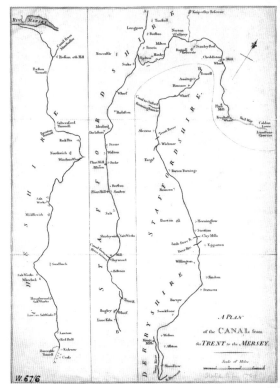

for Brindley and for engineering. Not only did the stone bridge stay up, but it held its water and man, it seemed, was able to defy the elements.

It was to be a defining moment. From that day on the doubters and naysayers were in retreat. This is not to say that they didn't continue to do all they could to try to strangle at birth this new phenomenon of inland waterways. Some objected on religious grounds, that it was blasphemous to alter God's order. Others objected on more practical grounds, either out of self interest for their land or the nation's interest, with one argument going that enticing men to artificial waterways would undermine the seafaring traditions of the Royal Navy. After the opening of the Barton Aqueduct and the completion of what was to become known as the Bridgewater Canal, it was clear where the future lay.

The canal had defied the odds. If it had not been for the particular combination of skills present in the triumvirate it is entirely possible that it would have failed. That and the convenient fact that the duke owned much of the land the canal traversed. Brindley had refused to give in to each

Horsepower in action.
(Courtesy of Phil Dowe)

new engineering challenge, whilst the duke had been prepared to practically bankrupt himself for the project and John Gilbert had managed the egos and practicalities involved with special flair. The whole enterprise had been completed in five years using basic technology such as picks and barrows, dependent on pure muscle power and, sometimes, pure instinct.

The price of coal into Manchester halved instantly and, perhaps just as importantly, security of supply was guaranteed, thus giving the owners of new steam engines the confidence to invest in the growing cotton industry. A sufficient and steady food supply was also secured, allowing the town to grow and supply the labour for the new industries.

Unsurprisingly, further schemes were mooted and another canal convert, who had followed progress in Worsley with a close personal interest, become involved. Thomas Wedgwood had based his pottery business around Stoke but faced two main problems: getting stocks of heavy china

The Exeter Ship Canal today. (Courtesy of Chris Reed)

clay to his potteries and getting his fragile finished goods out. A canal was the answer to both these problems, and so began the idea of the Trent and Mersey Canal, known at the time as the Grand Trunk, effectively linking the east and west coasts of the country via Stoke.

Brindley was appointed to the task, which immediately presented him with two more massive engineering problems. First, the Bridgewater had had no locks, whereas the Trent and Mersey, which went over the spine of the country, was going to need a lot of them. Second was the issue of Harecastle Hill outside Stoke, which was going to need a tunnel through it, a tunnel like the country had never seen before.

In the meantime, Wedgwood wasn't the only man demanding Brindley's services, and before long the engineer was heading up schemes across the country. As the opening of the Barton Aqueduct was to the Bridgewater, so completion of the tunnel at Harecastle became to the Trent and Mersey – its defining moment. Brindley was not to see that day though, dying five years before, in 1772, of late onset diabetes, possibly brought on by exhaustion.

At the time of his death Brindley had been engaged in trying to fulfil his vision of a 'Grand Cross' of canals, linking the four great seaports of London, Bristol, Liverpool and Hull, with the growing manufacturing centre of Birmingham at its core. While work continued on the canals connected to this idea in the years after Brindley's death, the momentum seemed to pale, resulting in a pause before the next great rush of activity.

Did you know?
The Mersey and Irwell Navigation was superseded by what became the Manchester Ship Canal, opened in 1894.

CANAL MANIA

Beyond the Bridgewater, James Brindley lived to see a few canals built in his lifetime. The most significant of these was the Staffordshire and Worcester, which was finished four months before his death. This canal was important, not just because of its length but because, along with a section connecting Stoke with the Trent on the still being built Trent and Mersey, it constituted one arm of Brindley's dream of a 'Grand

Wharfs, such as this one at Aynho on the South Oxford Canal, would be used to load and unload goods.

Banbury Lock, on the South Oxford Canal, linking Birmingham to London, via the Thames.

Did you know?
A boat going through a typical 'Brindley Lock' uses 30,000 gallons of water.

Cross', linking Bristol, via the Severn, with Liverpool.

Although the dream of a national transport system did not die with Brindley, it did lose some urgency. Always free with his knowledge, Brindley left behind a small cadre of canal engineers capable of continuing his work, but progress slowed. Canals he'd been associated with were eventually completed, but often some years after he'd gone. The Oxford Canal, for example, which was to provide the link to London via the Thames, was not finished until 1790, as was the Coventry. The Leek branch of the Caldon Canal he'd been working on when he died was only opened in 1802.

Not only had the canals lost their champion, but the economic backdrop had worsened considerably, largely due to

The Grand Union Canal provided a quicker route between London and the nation's second city.

The Grand Union had a number of 'arms' linking it to towns on its route.

constraints brought about by the American Civil War. The next phase of canal building, known as 'canal mania', had to wait until the last decade of the century. Another war, this one against Napoleon, was again causing damage to the economy, but wider forces were at work which came together to build an irresistible pressure to reinvigorate the vision of building a coherent transport infrastructure linking the main parts of the country.

Towards the end of the century the pace of population shift away from the countryside and into the towns really began to take off, as did the move towards more of a manufacturing-based economy. The ability to move troops around the country with greater ease also held attractions. At

Interesting canal architecture at Gailey Wharf on the Staffordshire and Worcester Canal, which was finished just before James Brindley's death.

Gargrave on the Leeds and Liverpool Canal marks the most northerly point of the modern system in England.

pressures attention turned back to the potential of the canals.

The success of the Trent and Mersey Canal in particular offered an exemplar. Not only did it show that canals could be profitable, but its model of funding, recognisable today as a joint stock company with individuals owning shares which then paid dividends related to profits, showed how the necessary funds could be raised. Canals became the most fashionable investment around. In 1790 one canal had been authorised by Parliament, but by 1793, when the mania peaked, this had risen to twenty.

What followed was a classic bubble, recognisable to more modern eyes as something akin to the 'dot com' boom at the turn of the millennium. Ideas were put forward and achieved funding more because they

the same time, a run of good harvests after 1783 had allowed many to accumulate personal wealth with no obvious places to invest it in. Under these combined

Hawkesbury Junction, or 'Sutton's Stop', where the Trent and Mersey and North Oxford canals meet.

Did you know?
Such was the trade on the Trent and Mersey that a second Harecastle Tunnel was dug under the guidance of Thomas Telford, which is still used today.

met the current fashion than any sensible financial rationale. Although not all the schemes that got parliamentary approval, or even funding, were built, a large number did, and by the dawn of the new century a rash of new canals covered the land.

A good example of a 'broadening', with a wide lock living alongside a disused narrow one.

conceived. Almost without exception over their lifetimes these canals were to each suffer from decisions made in haste, or as a result of under-investment, or lack of expertise.

A good example of this was the 'Grand Junction' Canal, a key component of what was increasingly being regarded as 'the system', which provided an alternative to the river-dependent Oxford Canal linking Birmingham and London. The section from Brentford in London to Braunston in the Midlands was built as a 'broad' canal, that is wide enough to take cargo-carrying craft up to 14ft in width heading in each direction. The section from Braunston into Birmingham, however, was built as a 'narrow' canal, offering passage only to more traditional narrow boats, which were half the width.

With each passing year the country's canal map grew ever more complex, but behind the scenes there were problems. The new canals never quite shook off the economic constraints in which they were

Elsewhere, canals were built with the aim more of joining two points on the map together rather than obeying more basic economic drivers such as access. Although initial resistance to canals in town centres from landowners contributed to this, the result was a later rush to add 'arms' to main canals, providing spurs to where industry and markets actually lay.

Despite these difficulties, many of the canals built during this period did provide their shareholders with good returns. In some cases rates of return were for a time as high as 25 per cent, and in the exceptional case of the Loughborough Canal reached the giddy heights of 150 per cent per annum. In the latter example this was because the canal was, in effect, the only option in a particular situation, in Loughborough's case hauling coal.

Napton, where a windmill looks down on the canal.

Did you know?
Canals were often designed to meander for miles around a contour to avoid the expense of building a lock or digging a tunnel.

Norton Junction, at the start of the Leicester Arm off the Grand Union Canal.

The roads remained poor and the rivers stubbornly continued to flow only where nature intended.

For those with sufficiently attuned ears, however, there was a distant sound on the horizon, one that would contrast sharply

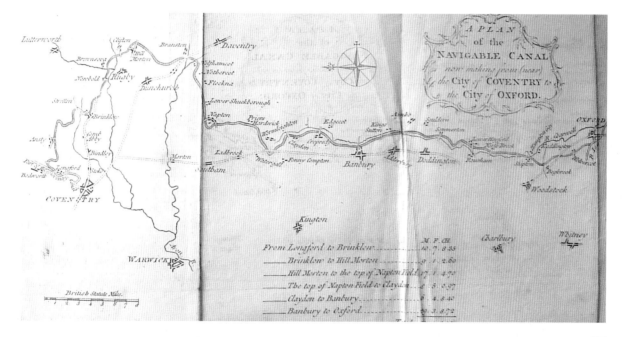

A classic 'Brindley Lock'.

and reliability and one powered not by horses, but by a new device born of man's ingenuity: the steam engine.

In 1825 a twenty-six-mile-long railway was opened, linking Stockton and Darlington, capable of taking coal from various collieries to the sea. Significantly, the route had initially been considered for a canal, but the new railway had won out. Equally significantly, the railway began to run a passenger service. Everything was about to change.

with the relative silence of the waterways. This sound was being made by a new rival, one able to provide greater flexibility, speed

At this point in the narrowboat story it is worth pausing to consider some of the men whose efforts brought about the canals. Amongst these there were the leaders, the engineers whose energy and inventiveness allowed the routes to be surveyed, the natural obstacles to be overcome and the practical difficulties thought through: the 'canal heroes'. Then there were the 'unsung heroes', the men whose muscle power and sweat allowed the imaginings of the engineers to become a reality: the 'navvies'.

Following James Brindley's untimely demise a small cadre of fellow-enthusiasts remained to keep his vision of a 'Grand Cross' alive. Amongst these were former assistants such as Robert Whitworth, who worked on the Birmingham, Oxford and Coventry canals; Samuel Weston, who constructed the Chester Canal and also worked on the Oxford; and Samuel Simcock, who worked with Brindley on the Staffordshire and Worcester.

Another contemporary was John Smeaton (1724–1792), justifiably known as the 'father of civil engineering'; it was he who marked the distinction between military and non-military engineering. An example of the sort of polymath that seemed to define these times, amongst his

◄ James Smeaton is sometimes known as 'The Father of Civil Engineering'.

◄◄ A polymath, Telford was the undisputed king of the second wave of canal building.

The southern portal of the Blisworth Tunnel.

The cast-iron aqueduct at Cosgrove over the River Great Ouse.

many achievements Smeaton could include designing the third Eddystone Lighthouse (still visible, although re-erected, at Plymouth Hoe), inventing modern cement and devising a water engine for the Royal Botanic Gardens in Kew. On top of

this, Smeaton was involved in a number of waterways projects, many of which involved improvements to navigations, including the Calder and Hebble and the River Lee.

As Brindley had his assistants, so did Smeaton, and perhaps the one who went on to the greatest prominence in his own right was William Jessop (1745–1814), who cut his teeth on the Grand Canal of Ireland. In 1789 Jessop was appointed the Chief Engineer to the Cromford Canal linking the River Derwent with the Erewash Canal. This project included the Derwent Viaduct, which unfortunately collapsed in 1793. A highly modest man, Jessop shouldered the blame for this calamity and had it repaired at his own expense.

Jessop's greatest achievement was undoubtedly the Grand Junction Canal linking Birmingham and London. This canal, now known as the Grand Union, is important to our story not only because of the two points it linked, but also because it included two significant tunnels, at Blisworth and Braunston, as well as an aqueduct at Wolverton to carry the canal over the River Great Ouse. Like that at Derwent, however, in 1808 this too failed and three years later was replaced with an iron version, known as the Cosgrove Aqueduct. Jessop's modesty may help to explain his relative lack of notoriety, although his contribution to the canal system was significant.

A contemporary of Jessop's whose reputation has proven to have greater staying power was Thomas Telford (1757–1834) – indeed, Jessop provided Telford with advice on his very first waterways

project, the Ellesmere Canal in 1793. Like Brindley, Telford was born into a modest rural family, spent his early years as an apprentice and had his career boosted by a wealthy patron, in this case Sir William Pulteney, at one time the country's richest man, but now perhaps better remembered by the bridge that bears his name in Bath.

Telford seemed to have better luck with aqueducts than Jessop, and was responsible for the system's finest, the cast-iron Pontcysyllte over the River Dee in the Vale of Llangollen, constructed in 1805. In fact, so successful was he that this material and design was used for the Cosgrove Aqueduct on Jessop's Grand Junction. Other Telford landmarks on the system include the Birmingham and Liverpool section of the Shropshire Canal and the Caledonian Canal in Scotland. More than just a canal engineer,

Telford was also instrumental in constructing new highways, including sections of the London to Holyhead road.

Another of Telford's feats was overseeing the second tunnel at Harecastle. Whereas Brindley's tunnel had taken eleven years to bore, Telford managed the 2,897 yards in only three. What was more, unlike Brindley's, Telford's tunnel had a towpath, allowing horses to pull the boats, although it was still only wide enough to allow for one-way traffic.

Although the ingenuity of the engineers behind these feats is indisputable, they still needed to be built. Here our story turns to the 'navvies', the men who constructed both these and the actual canals themselves. Once the course of a canal was decided it was the job of these men to physically apply the picks and shovels required to move the

◄ Muscle power, picks and barrows still helped cut the canals even 100 years after the first canals, as seen here in the cutting of the Manchester Ship Canal. (Courtesy of Frank Mullineux Collection, Salford City Council)

▲ The Pontcysyllte Aqueduct on the Llangollen Canal. (Courtesy of British Waterways)

Did you know?
The word 'navvy', meaning any general labourer, originated from the canal 'navigators'.

earth. Working in gangs, with spoil carried away in nothing more sophisticated than a wooden hand barrow, the men rarely knew what they'd encounter, rocks, different types of soil and tree roots, all of which had to be shifted.

of the task remained based upon raw manpower. At first, 'navvies' were recruited from the locale, and would return to the land when the canal was finished; but in time some decided to stay in the canal business and moved from one job to the next. Wages were meagre (no more than

The Globe Inn at Leighton Buzzard, an archetypal canal pub.

Pausing at Braunston.

Once a decent length had been completed water would be let in and spoil might then be taken away by boat, but the essence

◄◄ *Old and new, two old working boats in the foreground and some hotel boats on the opposite bank.*

◄ *Harecastle Tunnel from the north, showing two entrances, Telford's on the left and Brindley's on the right.*

Did you know?

Most tunnels lacked a towpath, which meant that boats had to be 'legged' along the length, a process which required lying sideways on a plank and literally 'walking' the boat along the sides of the tunnel.

1s 6d a day in 1770), and much of that was spent on food and ale – although the canal companies could be surprisingly generous in providing the latter. At the height of 'canal mania' it is estimated around 50,000 men were digging canals, not only the routes themselves, but also the deep locks and their accompanying chambers.

Once the channel had, quite literally, been cut there was another task. The sides of the canal had to be made watertight, a process that required lining them with loam and clay, a process known as 'puddling'. A dirty job at the best of times (the layer could be anything between eighteen inches and a yard thick), navvies were often called into service to stamp the puddle down using their feet. Only if they were lucky would herds of local livestock be called into action instead.

Navvies worked hard and played hard, and the coming of a canal to a previously quiet rural hamlet could have the same effect as a swarm of locusts on a ripe field. Publicans may have cheered their arrival, but decent womenfolk and farmers must have dreaded them, the only reassurance being that their stay would be temporary.

But the canals themselves would normally outlive those who lived near them when they were being dug. Once a canal had come to your area nothing would ever be the same again. Not only would you have a means of easily getting to bigger villages or towns, but the sheer fact of strangers passing regularly through would transmit news and gossip, changing the way of rural life forever.

Starting the hard physical task of 'legging' through a tunnel. In reality, leggers would lie flat as they worked their way down the tunnel. (Courtesy of Stuart Coleman © 2011)

Did you know?

The canals ushered in a consumer age – for the first time ordinary people could afford ceramic plates rather than wooden platters as well as metal cutlery.

WORKING THE CANALS

One sure-fire way to annoy a narrowboater is to call his boat a 'barge'. Narrowboats are just that, no more than 7ft wide, whereas barges are twice as broad. Don't worry too much if you do give offence though, for narrowboaters have their own vocabulary of terms they use to describe other craft, and these are not always complimentary. Perhaps the most disparaging of these are 'noddy boat', a general term of derision for a pleasure craft, or 'plastic boat' for anything made of resin.

The reason narrowboats are narrow is highly practical. Given the expense associated with cutting a canal, early versions tended to be no wider than absolutely necessary, and although the Trent and Mersey offered a wider model, suitable for barges, it was not always taken up.

Early boats tended to echo the shapes and designs of craft from the local area, whether river or coastal craft, such as the keel, a form of boat typical of Yorkshire and the River Humber, characterised by round middles and almost flat fronts. Mersey flats from the Dee, Weaver, Mersey and Irwell rivers, had a round bilge and two masts, and it was these sorts of boats that featured on early etchings of the opening of the Barton Aqueduct.

Two other forms were the trow, a type of barge popular on the River Severn and the coastal waters of the south west, defined by open holds with extra canvas bulwarks laced up to a rail, along with carvel-style hulls; and the Thames Barge. The latter were defined by large tan-coloured sails and flat bottoms, with masts and leeboards that could be raised or lowered,

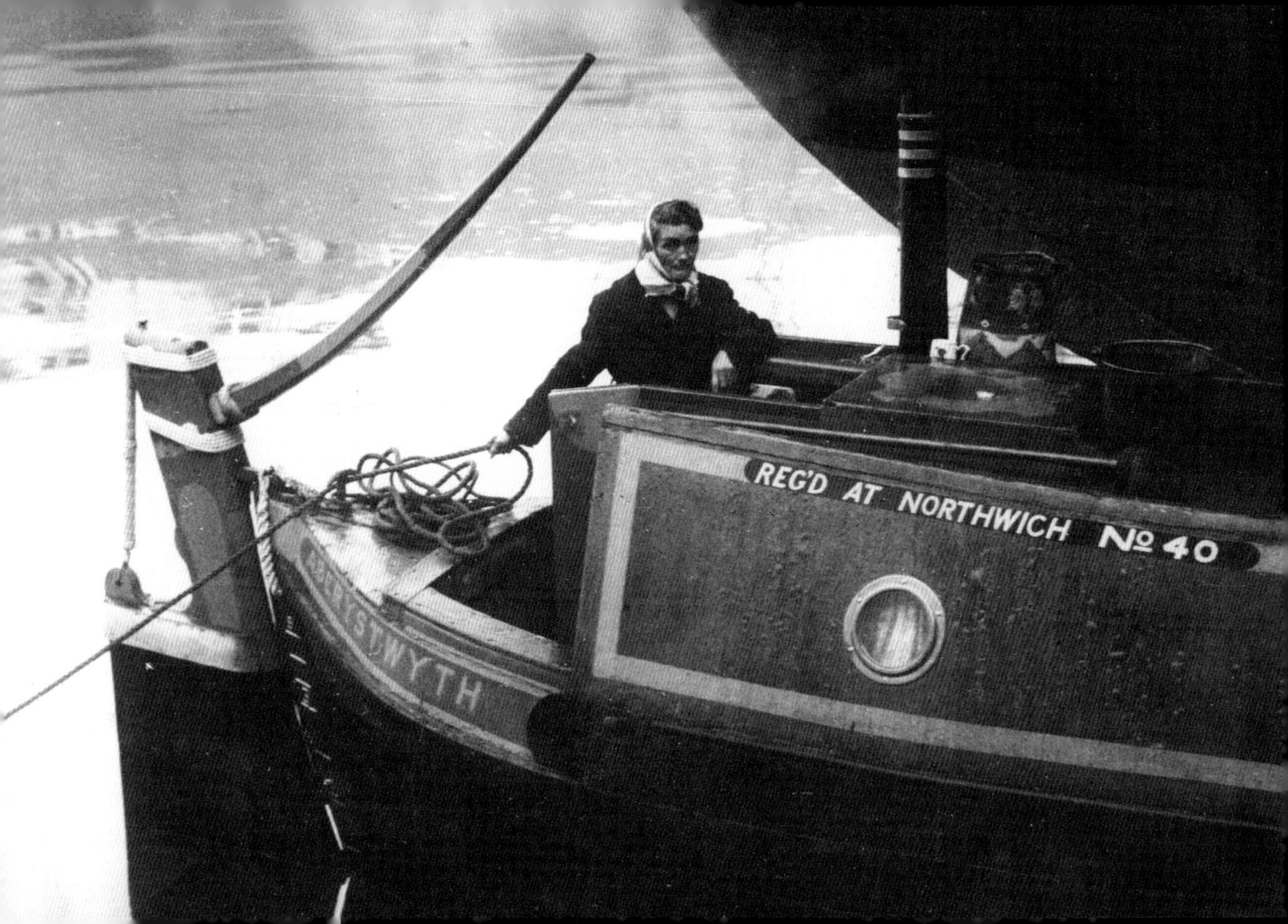
REG'D AT NORTHWICH №40

A barge, updated with the addition of solar panels.

Did you know?

Keels were not dissimilar in shape to the longboats used by the Vikings, which may go some way to explain another term used by the uninitiated to describe canal craft.

making them highly manoeuvrable along the crowded waters of the capital's river.

This tradition of local influence continued as boats began to be purpose built. The vast majority of these were constructed from wood, and although some, such as John 'Iron Mad' Wilkinson, experimented with iron, wood was easier to patch and carpenters easier to come by. The main stylistic differences lay with the hull, with the consideration of whether or not living space was required determining a V or a U shape.

The best example of a local style was the 'Josher', named after Joshua Fellows of the cargo carrying company Fellows, Morton & Clayton. Joshua spotted an opportunity when the Grand Junction Canal Company went under in 1876, buying up their boats and building his own. These were a compromise between iron and wood, with a riveted wrought-iron side and a three-inch elm bottom. With the coming of steam, coke boilers were installed, which although they cut down on cargo space did add enough power for one boat to pull another, with unpowered craft known as 'buttys'.

Steam never really replaced horsepower; it took diesel to do that, the coming of which necessitated another design shift.

With efficiency dictating the need to have the engine as close to the propeller as possible, the cabin space, already restricted, became even more so. It is from this necessity that the extremely cramped living quarters associated with cargo-carrying

▲ Trade continues today on the canals, even if the goods being traded may have changed!

narrowboats comes. As economic pressures grew narrowboat men brought their wives and children on board to help, leading to whole families living in a space that was, quite literally, too small to swing a cat in.

Life may have been hard, but it was proud (see opposite on Roses and Castles). Narrowboatmen saw themselves as superior to those simply working the barges, so it is perhaps with some irony that they became known as 'bargees', reinforcing the common confusion between the two terms. Children lived a peripatetic existence with days of school snatched where they could be found and everyone and everything existing with a keen sense of space.

These days narrowboats fall into three broad styles reflecting modern leisure

on a space no wider than a foot. The cruiser takes its name from river cruisers and has large open decks both fore and aft, often with the luxuries of a rail and seating. Here, interior space is sacrificed for somewhere to sit and greater freedom to move for the helmsman. The third style is the semi-trad, a compromise, where the hatch and doors are placed forward but the sides are stretched to provide more protected seating and some shelter at the back.

ROSES AND CASTLES

For the first hundred years of the canals most boats were painted black. In time, however, the practical virtues of a splash of colour led to more brightly painted craft. Bold primary colours are easier to spot on a dull day against black water, and as it was often dark inside a cabin the benefits

◄ Castles, roses and a lace window decoration.

Did you know?
Steam craft became known as 'fly boats', because they could work 'fly' i.e. both day and night, unlike horses.

usage, although the need to be careful with space remains. The first style is the trad or traditional, with a small unguarded deck at the back where the helmsman often stands

Even doorbells can be painted.

The Grand Union Canal Carrying Company kept the flag flying for freight on the canals.

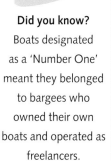

Did you know?

Boats designated as a 'Number One' meant they belonged to bargees who owned their own boats and operated as freelancers.

of having coloured utensils and other belongings were obvious. In time, these possessions also became a matter of pride to the wives working the boats, giving lie to the popular misconception that boatpeople were somehow second class.

At first decoration was very basic, geometric shapes or stripes, as painting was

Canalware makes for popular souvenirs.

A Leeds and Liverpool 'short' barge, i.e. only 60ft long.

Narrowboat cabins were and are extremely cramped.

➤➤ Shrewley Tunnel on the Grand Union has a separate entrance for horses.

Painted baths.

➤➤ Narrowboat and Barge – don't confuse the two!

limited to time when a boat was laid up for maintenance. In time, narrowboats became synonymous with Roses and Castles, a motif that is deceptively simple, capable of having its base laid down by an apprentice and the finishing touches applied by a more skilled painter. The disappointing thing is no one really knows why this style came about. The most likely explanation is that it links back to the 'teaboard' style, popular on biscuit tins and other metal objects at the time, or possibly there are links back to folk or Romany art, although this is speculation. Another theory evokes the nineteenth-century revival of all things Gothic.

Pride of place usually went to the Buckby Bucket, often placed strategically on a boat's roof. This also had a practical use as the boat's main water container, and as such was one of the most important and personal possessions a family could have.

◄ A Fellows, Morton & Clayton working boat outside the Black Country Living Museum. (Courtesy of Beddard/ Dudley Public Libraries)

Did you know?
Children growing up on boats often 'learned their numbers' from playing cards, hence the popularity of card suits as decoration on boats.

Basic geometric designs brighten up a working boat.

The year 1845 marked the high point of the canals, with over 4,400 miles of navigable waterway, three quarters of which was linked to the network. The same year also represented the tipping point at which power shifted towards rail. If the growth of the canals had been impressive, it was nothing compared to the railways. The first crude railway between Stockton and Darlington had been opened only twenty years before, but by 1845 a quarter of the canal companies had been sold to their tracked rivals.

The heyday of the canals was short but impressive. Canal companies had been paying good dividends right through the 1830s and, as we have seen, money was still being poured into them; and grand schemes such as Telford's second Harecastle Tunnel were underway. The reality was, however, that canals could not compete economically with the railways. What happened next was a long and at times desperate fight for survival.

The Grand Union Canal is usefully marked out with milestones.

A horse-drawn butty being hauled between locks. (Courtesy of James Payler, Blisworth Images)

Did you know?

Like the 'Land Girls' who worked the farms, a cadre of women operated canal boats during the Second World War, known as 'Idle Women'.

Whereas once all the smart money had been directed towards canal schemes, it was now the new railway companies that attracted any available investment funds. The motives of these companies in buying up their water-based rivals were mixed. Some had ambitions to create what we might call today an 'integrated transport network', with transfer stations capable of taking goods to or from boats and rail wagons according to which was most efficient. Others were more ruthless, taking the canals over simply to close them down, for their land (like canals, railways favoured 'flat' routes) or to use as

President and *Kildare*. *President was built in 1909 for £600 by Fellows Morton & Clayton, now restored and an attraction at the Black Country Living Museum.*

Here, outside Warwick, the canal passes over a railway on an aqueduct.

a decent solution to the problems of the latter part of the eighteenth century, were not able to meet the demands of the nineteenth. The speed, load-carrying capacity and efficiency of the railways simply could not be matched.

Still, the canals tried to adapt to survive. Steam tugs were introduced in the 1860s and, as we saw in the previous chapter, engines subsequently reduced enough in size to allow one boat to pull a butty, doubling the cargo a boatman could control. The turn of the nineteenth century saw the introduction of diesel engines, although these were not the relatively easy machines we know today and required considerable skill to start up and keep going. Ironically though, as the engines improved so they made road transport a more viable proposition.

bargaining chips to restrict the growth of rival railway companies.

During the height of the canal boom the country had changed beyond recognition. There had been a massive shift of population into the towns, and factories had become commonplace. The canals,

Both part of a big re-ordering of boats by the Grand Union Canal Carrying Company in 1935, Scorpio and Malus worked until nationalisation. Subsequently restored, both are now recognised as National Historic Ships.

Did you know?

A typical cabin on a working narrowboat measures around 9ft by 7ft.

It was during this long slow period of decline that bargees brought their families onto the boats in order to save on paying rent. Boatmen were paid by miles travelled and load carried and for some a decent living was possible, but they were the exception rather than the rule. Boating was for many families a way of life; they simply

65

A weighing machine at Stoke Bruerne canalside village and museum.

Once highly successful, the Somerset Coal Canal was a victim of the railways.

knew nothing else. Meanwhile, even the government, it seemed, were on their backs, with legislation introduced in the 1880s demanding a separate cabin for children, often located at the front of the boat, cutting down on cargo capacity.

All was not gloom and doom, however, and around this time the Manchester Ship Canal was dug, linking Manchester and Liverpool, although this was a different beast altogether from the sorts of waters a narrowboat would ply, being capable of taking ocean-going craft. Other improvements and canal arms were also added to the system, such as the Anderton Lift and the Foxton Inclined Plane, both ingenious engineering solutions to particular problems. In the case of the former, this took the form of a 'boat elevator', capable of transferring boats between the Trent and Mersey and the River Weaver.

Despite the range of forces stacked up against them the canals proved to be remarkably resilient, and gained a further stay of execution with the two world wars when all available national resources were pressed into action. Between the wars desperate levels of unemployment also saw the canals benefitting from work creation schemes, the most high-profile example being the creation, and subsequent widening of, the Grand Union Canal in the 1920s and '30s, bringing together waterways both broad and narrow into a single and consistent route connecting London and Birmingham.

By this time, however, it wasn't the railways the canals had to worry about so much as the roads. Government intervention of a different kind was the next significant moment in the network's history when, in 1948, they became part of the British Transport Commission, part of a grand plan to provide 'an efficient, adequate, economic and properly integrated system of public inland transport and port facilities within Great Britain for passengers and goods.' In other words, the canals were nationalised; although in a twist of irony they were accompanied in the Commission by the 'Big Four' railway companies and 246 road haulage firms.

Did you know?
Early diesel engines required a handle and a blow torch to warm up the fuel to start them up – not easy outdoors on a cold day in January!

The canals may have been nationalised, but no one really knew what to do with them. Trade had all but disappeared and to live near one was seen to be a sign of misfortune – they smelt, looked ugly and were often 'downright dangerous', especially to young children in a time when entertaining yourself meant wandering about the countryside rather than staying inside attached to a computer. Drownings were not uncommon, and calls were often made to fill them in permanently, and not just with shopping trolleys and rubbish.

At this point in the narrowboat story some unlikely saviours appear on the scene. Principal amongst them was a jobless vintage car enthusiast who set out with his new wife in the summer 1939 to cruise the inland waterways in his boat *Cressy*. The journey was published as *Narrow Boat* in 1944, raising awareness of the state of the canals and their potential. Two other enthusiasts, Robert Aickman and Charles Hadfield, read the book and joined

Did you know?

During the late 1990s more miles of canal were being re-opened per year than were being built at the height of canal mania.

▶ **Opposite top row, left to right:** *Family holidaying on the Staffordshire and Worcestershire Canal.*

▶ *Sharing a lock at Stoke Bruerne.*

▶ *Taking it easy on the Lapworth flight, Stratford Canal.*

▶ **Middle row, left to right:** *Not all canals are narrow – Tixal Wide on the Staffordshire and Worcestershire Canal.*

▶ *Stourport, where the River Severn meets the canal.*

▶ *Approaching a pub on the Staffordshire and Worcestershire Canal.*

▶ **Bottom row, left to right:** *The Blue Lias Inn at Stockton on the Grand Union Canal.*

▶ *A rare pair of working boats on the Grand Union at Braunston in the early 1990s.*

TOP LOCK, STOKE BRUERNE, GRAND UNION CANAL

LAPWORTH FLIGHT, STRATFORD CANAL

TIXALL WIDE, STAFFS AND WORCS CANAL

THE BOAT INN, STOCKTON, GRAND UNION CANAL

Once the site of a major rally to save the canals, Banbury now holds an annual canal and music festival. (Courtesy of Allan Ford)

Rolt on a second voyage and together, in 1946, to set up the Inland Waterways Association (IWA), dedicated to preserving the waterways.

The 1950s were characterised by active campaigning, with mass boat rallies at key spots on the system in danger. One such, at Banbury, was organised to draw attention to plans to fill in the canal in order to build a bus station, an action that would

have killed the Oxford Canal by cutting off access to the Thames. During this time IWA members succeeded as acting as friends

Caen Hill flight on the Kennet and Avon Canal, one of the big success stories of the canal renaissance.

Birmingham and the Birmingham Canal Navigations lie at the heart of the canal network.

➤ In the 1990s there was even talk of brand new waterways being cut, not just restoring old ones.

Did you know?

Half the population of the UK lives within five miles of a British Waterways canal or river.

of, and advocates for, the canals where previously there had been none, buying time for a rethink on their future role.

At the same time, volunteers began to come together to restore dying canals, in an attempt to turn round the momentum. It was clear that trade wasn't the answer and as the economy got going again it became equally clear that there might be a place for the canals to act as a leisure resource. Meanwhile, in 1957, the government set up the Bowes Committee to review the waterways system, and although the committee's conclusions were inconclusive they were enough to spare the canals from a Beeching-like rationalisation.

In 1963 the British Waterways Board was established with a clear remit to promote leisure use, designating a number of canals as 'cruising waterways'. At the same time enthusiasts for particular canals formed individual canal societies, for both existing and unnavigable waterways. Their first success was the re-opening of the Stratford Canal from Lapworth south to Stratford in 1964, after which the National Trust took up the cause. Further restorations followed, including the Ashton and Peak

Forest Canals in 1974 and, eventually, the Kennet and Avon Canal linking Reading and Bath, opened by HM the Queen in 1990.

Perhaps the most significant sign of the shift in attitudes towards the canals was the approach taken first in Birmingham and

L.T.C. Rolt's book Narrow Boat was seminal in the formation of the Inland Waterways Association.

Lobbying for the canals was widespread when they were threatened by massive cuts.

later in Manchester and other towns and cities. What was once seen as a liability became seen as a potential asset, with the Gas Street Basin complex in the heart of Birmingham being transformed into an iconic feature of that city. This shift was sealed when in the 1990s Banbury itself

STANDEDGE VISITOR CENTRE
Gateway to Standedge Tunnel
- the highest, longest and deepest canal tunnel in Britain
opened 25th May 2001
by Lily Turner, daughter of David Whitehead
the fastest legger through the tunnel in 1914

This stone was donated by
Johnsons Wellfield Quarries Ltd

Standedge Tunnel, the
longest on the system and
yet another restoration
success story. (Courtesy
of British Waterways)

Did you know?
Standedge has the
distinction of being
the highest, longest
and deepest tunnel on
the waterways system
and is three and a
quarter miles long.

finally got its new bus station – alongside the canal, which became a feature of a new shopping complex.

Through the latter half of the twentieth century the canals found their new role, with many families enjoying a holiday in their own country, drifting slowly through the countryside. Such was the change in mood that people began to look not just towards keeping the system but to expanding it. Canal societies that had literally laboured away in evenings and weekends were about to get a lucky break: the National Lottery.

Well organised, with a good cause and the ability to appeal to both heritage and future sentiments, the canal societies were ideally positioned to pitch for funds, and they succeeded. In the years either side of the millennium over £190 million of lottery funds was won for waterways projects. Suddenly, the talk was not just of restorations but of creating brand new waterways, most notably a fifteen-mile link between the Grand Union at Milton Keynes and the River Great Ouse in Bedford.

In the meantime other successes were chalked up – the re-opening of the Huddersfield Narrow Canal in 2001, which included the Standedge Tunnel, and of the Rochdale Canal the following year. In all, over 200 miles of waterway were re-introduced to the system during this time and just as importantly, British Waterways (as it now was) was able to catch up on its maintenance backlog. In 2005 British Waterways issued a policy document setting out its vision of 'a network that will be used by twice as many people in 2012 as had used it ten years previously'. It was canal mania all over again, but like canal mania, it could not last.

In August 2006 funding difficulties in DEFRA, the government department responsible for the waterways, initiated a massive round of cost cutting, and the

Did you know?
British Waterways and its joint venture partners are currently working on more than seventy waterway regeneration schemes worth £10 billion.

canals weren't exempt. Fresh rallies were organised, including one in Gas Street Basin underneath the television studio where the relevant minister was giving an interview, and for a time the future, once so bright, began to look very bleak indeed.

With hindsight, it's possible to see this shock as a pre-credit crunch wake-up call. The waterways did not go under, and in 2009 British Waterways put forward a plan to move into the third sector by becoming a charitable trust, a move confirmed in the 2010 budget. As part of this plan Local Partnership Boards are envisaged with the intention of giving local people more say in the running of the waterways.

It's almost as if the waterways had been having so much fun that they hadn't seen the cliff edge coming. Having just stopped in time and having looked over that edge

they have re-grouped. Once more the future horizon looks positive, perhaps not quite so sunny as it once seemed, but certainly more sustainable.

▲ *Two motorised boats from the Willow Wren Canal Carrying Company around 1955. (Courtesy of T.W. King Collection, Dudley Archives)*

LIVING ABOARD

Narrowboats have found a new role, and whilst these days most people associate them with holidays (covered in the next chapter), for many thousands of people they represent a home.

The prospect of escaping the rat race and embracing a life afloat, to become a liveaboard as they are known, can be an alluring one; but as with so many things in life, the reality doesn't always match the dream. Yes, it's a simpler life, but it's a different one too, one involving compromises and sometimes difficult choices, requiring a shift in mindset if the fantasy isn't to become a nightmare.

Almost by definition, liveaboards choose to take on responsibility for many of the facets of modern civilised life the rest of us regard as givens. Amongst these are access to services such as on-demand electricity, gas, water, sewerage, telephone and even broadband. Whether moored or moving, boat-dwellers have to proactively seek out services that arrive automatically into a bricks and mortar home.

Solving these problems requires foresight and planning, with the monitoring and

Solar energy can help make a boat less reliant on battery power.

replenishing of basics such as energy and water key liveaboard skills. Living on board a boat is a bit like having your own cocoon or life-support mechanism, requiring constant checking. For many this is part of the attraction; it certainly makes them more conscious of their impact upon the planet and what it takes to sustain a reasonable standard of living. Perhaps

△ Accidents can, and do, happen!

◁ Just because it's a boat doesn't mean it can't be comfortable.

literally, 'of no fixed abode' – and all this implies. Modern bureaucracy doesn't tend to cope well with this concept and it's here that the clever liveaboard learns how to out-smart 'the system'.

Collecting post from friends, family or friendly marinas is an option for some but a permanent solution is preferable, such as a hosting address or a PO Box. Part of the attraction of a life afloat may be the option to escape junk mail, along with the argument that in the world of the internet physical letters are 'so last century'. That is, of course, until the reality of patchy internet access and dropped phone signals in a field in the middle of nowhere hits home.

Banks also tend to have a problem with people of 'no fixed abode' and liveaboards have to create their own version of offshore banking, ideally before they cast off their

equally attractive, it helps them re-define what 'reasonable' means in this context.

Tackling the less tangible aspects of being a liveaboard can be trickier. Whilst not everyone moves around most do, and it's at this point that they become, quite

that tends to equate 'no fixed abode' with 'non-person'. Hospitals will of course admit emergencies, but managing chronic complaints or accessing a GP if something flares up can be a problem for the liveaboard. Drop-in clinics help, as does knowing where they are in advance. Similar considerations also have to be given to accessing other parts of the welfare state such as pensions

◄ Living on board a boat can make city living affordable. (Courtesy of Allan Ford)

▼ Designs of boats can vary enormously, from the ornate to the functional.

ropes. Internet banking helps, if there's a connection, as do ATMs; but planning is again key here, and a fresh regard for the simplicities of cash also tends to resurface.

Strong organisational skills tend to characterise the successful liveaboard, but there are some things in life you cannot always plan for, and health is one of them. The NHS is another arm of 'the system'

including the most basic right of all, the right to vote. Boat dwellers are the ultimate floating voters, but our system links votes to geography, which can be tricky if you have consciously cut yourself adrift from land. Postal voting is an option, but again needs organising.

Being a citizen, floating or otherwise, also brings obligations, including the payment of taxes. Whilst the powers that be can be slow in allocating a vote, they tend to be a lot quicker when it comes to collecting taxes. Council Tax in particular is a bugbear for the liveaboard, not least due to different interpretations by different authorities. Liveaboards need to remind themselves that like the Mounties, HMRC always tends to get its man.

Living aboard involves a new set of rules for living and achieving a fresh balance –

Looks like this liveaboard is well stocked up for the winter.

A mini-palace on the Thames.

and social services, with liveaboards with pets or young children having another layer of considerations to contend with.

Liveaboards also have to make a conscious effort to maintain other rights,

> *Electricity hook ups can be a godsend for permanent boat dwellers. (Courtesy of Allan Ford)*

> *Not everyone is as tidy as the next man! (Courtesy of Allan Ford)*

Did you know?

Around 15,000 people live aboard a boat in the UK – that's twice the size of the average English town.

➤ *This run of liveaboard boats is immaculate.*

➤➤ *Living aboard means coping with everything the weather can throw at you! (Courtesy of Allan Ford)*

Did you know?

Special licences are available for constantly moving liveaboards that require them to prove they are on a 'continuous progressive journey', not staying in one spot for more than two weeks.

⯈ Wind turbines can also provide a useful 'top up'.

⯈⯈ Shelter whilst working; he's having a 'busy day'.

some things are sacrificed, but others are gained. The secret to liveaboard success lies with the three 'A's: accepting these rules, adopting a new mentality and adapting to suit individual needs and desires.

Did you know?

There are dedicated residential moorings on the canals and in marinas for those happier to have a more permanent base.

As Ratty so accurately observes in Kenneth Grahame's *Wind in the Willows*, there is 'absolutely nothing half as much fun as simply messing about in boats'. Although written a hundred years ago, this sentiment still seems to hold true for large sections of the UK population, many of whom opt for the perceived serenity and slower pace of a canal holiday.

Narrowboat holidays have in many ways been the saviour of the canals, enjoyed both by those who simply hire a boat for a

Did you know?
One hundred and fifty thousand people a year enjoy a canal holiday on the UK's inland waterways.

◀ *Now and then the waterways can get busy! (Courtesy of Allan Ford)*

89

▶ *Canal holidays are a popular choice for pet owners.*

Did you know?
There are 2,200 miles of navigable inland waterways, so there's plenty to choose from.

week or two or those lucky enough to own their own. From being, quite literally, the workhorses of the Industrial Revolution, the canals have transformed into a vital leisure resource – born in the eighteenth century, but very much part of the twenty-first too.

◄ The rule is, keep other boats to the left when passing.

91

Hotel Boats are another option for a canal holiday – let someone else take the strain!

Canals offer a rural idyll.

Renting a narrowboat is an ideal way to sample the inland waterways network, and whilst the basic experience may be common, such is the variety within the network that no two holidays need be the same. A number of things lie at the heart of a narrowboat holiday, with the 4mph speed limit on the canals ensuring that a slower pace is one of them. There are others too, however, including the ability to get closer to nature, to bond with friends and family in a relatively confined space and the opportunity to flex your muscles in the open air.

Narrowboat holidays aren't all gentle gliding and the occasional cold beer though; making your way along the waterways can involve considerable hard graft, and as with all things, a little forward planning can go a long way to ensuring everyone enjoys their holiday.

Here are seven top tips for a successful canal holiday:

1. Plan Ahead – Choose routes carefully. Do you want industrial heritage or rural rambling? Do you fancy tying up in the

Queues can form at some locks, throwing schedules awry – best not to have one in the first place.

heart of a major city for a while? Circular routes offer the most variety, but after the halfway point you are on a schedule and there's nothing relaxing about dawn to dusk no-stops cruising to get back to base on time.

2. Do the Maths – There may be a 4mph limit, but you'll be lucky to achieve 3. Plus you have to allow at least fifteen minutes per lock, assuming there's no queue. Consider how long you want to spend cruising each day and then knock a bit off for stops, rest and the unexpected. Six hours a day is enough for a sole helmsman, more than enough in a wet British summer!

3. Choose Your Craft – Narrowboats didn't get their name by chance. They may advertise themselves as sleeping six or eight, but maximum capacity can be a squeeze. Many see canal holidays as ideal

◄ *Sharing a lock saves water and effort.*

Did you know?
Approximately 35,000 leisure boats, including narrowboats and pleasure craft, and 30,000 canoeists, regularly take to the waters, which means the canals are actually busier than they were during their industrial peak!

for families; if so, is there somewhere for the kids to play during the day and settle down at night? Television or no? If there's a reliance on bunks will that suit everyone on board? Is there a sitting area at the front? Not all boats are the same.

▶ *Marinas and canalside shops make for convenient stopping places.*

▶▶ *Three abreast in a River Thames lock.*

▶▶ *Everyone was a learner some time!*

4. Take Control – A boat isn't a car; there are no brakes for one thing – the only way to stop is by throwing the boat into reverse and that tends to do strange things to the steering. What's more, even going forward can be tricky, especially when to turn left you need to send the rudder right.

5. Load Up, Load Up – Your boat is your life-support mechanism, but you need to strike a balance between stops and space. Some things will keep, like the Pinot Grigio, while others need to be bought more regularly, like bread and milk, and the fridge is unlikely to be of any great size. The golden rule with supplies is get them when you can and don't assume there will be another shop around the corner.

6. Moor the Merrier – The same 'assume the worst' philosophy can apply to mooring. Most holiday boats are too long to turn around and anyway, turning points tend to be few and far between. If you see a mooring point in the rough vicinity of where you want to be then take it – you can always move on later if you spot a better one, but you'll be stuck if there isn't

Crossing the Dundas Aqueduct on the Kennet and Avon Canal.

one at all. Choose your spot wisely though; a mooring outside a pub might seem a good idea at opening time, but less so at closing time.

7. Lock, Stock – Take time to understand the basic principle of locks, which is actually very simple. They can be dangerous places, especially for children and pets. Finally, try to avoid tying up if you're descending or you'll look a bit silly when the water disappears.

A final tip. Narrowboat holidays are very popular and the best craft tend to get booked up early, so plan ahead if you don't want to, quite literally, miss the boat!

As the canals contemplate their latest fresh dawn its worth pausing briefly to consider the full breadth of riches they bring to the nation. One way of doing this is to think of them as falling into three camps: reminders of our heritage, prompts to make us appreciate the here and now and prospects for the future.

As we have seen, the canals were forged in a time of colossal ambition and achievement, drawing in the leading engineering brains to create projects that were staggering in their audacity. Thanks largely to the efforts of the post-war enthusiasts many of these have survived to be marvelled at today. They range from bridges, tunnels, flights of locks and aqueducts to some of the less obvious, but still impressive, industrial architecture that lines the towpath, ranging from warehouses to pumping stations. Different canals also have their own trademark features, such as swing, lift and guillotine bridges, each providing their own challenge.

Some of the more monumental features have already received a mention in this story, such as the Barton Aqueduct and the Harecastle and Standedge Tunnels. Others on any discerning list would include the magnificent Caen Hill flight outside Devizes, a sequence of twenty-nine locks in less than two miles that lifts the Kennet and Avon Canal 237ft; along with the Bingley Five Rise on the Leeds and Liverpool Canal, which rises 59ft in just 320ft. The steepest flight of locks on the system, the Bingley Five Rise is a 'staircase', with the water from one emptying directly into the next, which means that boats proceeding through them have to exercise

Did you know?
British Waterways
is the largest owner
of listed buildings
in the UK after the
National Trust and the
Church of England,
responsible for
3,000 examples of
industrial heritage and
engineering feats.

◄ The canal can throw up some sudden surprises such as Cosgrove Bridge on the Grand Union, unique in being in the Gothic style.

Cropredy Lock on the South Oxford Canal, a perfect example of a lock cottage.

➤ *Ducklings resting on a rudder guard.*

➤➤ *Gloucester Historic Docks.*

a form of choreography that is fascinating to watch.

The Queen of Aqueducts is almost certainly the Pontcysyllte on the Llangollen Canal, although there are a number of others less extensive but still impressive along the system. Other marvels include the Foxton Inclined Plane on the Grand Union and the Anderton Boat Lift on the Trent and Mersey. These share the aim of transporting boats without resorting to locks, and whilst the former ultimately failed and is still under restoration, the latter succeeded and is now functioning again after a period of dereliction.

Perhaps some of the greatest pleasures to be derived from the canal system are features that might otherwise go past unnoticed, with the inevitably slower pace imposed by canal travel providing the

(513612)

COMFREY

CALCUTT

▶ This swing bridge on the Kennet and Avon Canal is handily placed across the middle of a lock.

▶▶ A canoeist glides across the water.

opportunity to enjoy a fresh perspective. Amongst these are the wide variety of flora and fauna available on view and a deeper appreciation of the passing of the seasons. Bird and insect life populate the silence, with the sight of a grey heron, as it awkwardly bursts into life and circles overhead, commonplace; whilst swans and various varieties of duck, along with their young, adopt a more graceful approach. Meanwhile, kaleidoscopic butterflies show off by demonstrating their ability to outpace a gently moving boat.

Toads, frogs, water voles, and yes the occasional rat, can also be seen in a real-life version of *Tales from the Riverbank*, and if you are in the right spot you may also spot an escaped mink. Time also allows deeper study of the banks, and many canal boats carry with them not only a guide

A lift bridge on the South Oxford Canal.

There are still plenty of canal treasures off the navigable system, such as this disused tunnel on the Thames and Severn Canal.

Time to adopt ...sion. (Courtesy ...d)

to native birds for identification purposes, but also a handbook of flower species. In these uncultivated spaces, away from the harmful spraying of pesticides, wild flowers flourish, from flag iris to marsh marigolds, mingling in amongst the more common rosebay willow herb, reeds and rushes.

Beneath the surface, of course, lie fish – from perch to roach, carp and chub, and maybe the occasional pike; and where there are fish there are also anglers. It is probably fair to say that boaters and fishermen often enjoy a strained relationship, with both feeling a sense of proprietorship over the water. In reality, a sense of begrudging truce prevails, with anglers reluctantly raising their rods to let boats go by and boaters frowning at rods lining a favoured mooring point.

Anglers are just one of the various other groups who enjoy our canals, with walkers, joggers, canoeists and cyclists all frequent visitors enjoying what the canals have to offer. Slowing down, being outdoors, seeing the country from a fresh angle, these are all some of the less tangible pleasures the canals provide; and although their interests may sometimes collide there is a sense of shared, if fleeting, camaraderie; experienced perhaps on the towpath at the end of the day or when sharing a lock, or in one of the many canalside pubs.

Having been rescued and redefined as a leisure resource, the canals and the boats that ply them undoubtedly have a future. The authorities set up to protect their interests and run them might come and go, but over the years they have shown a remarkable ability to flex and meet new opportunities.

With an eye to the future, potential has been spotted to use the towpaths as

Did you know?
Thirteen million people, or a quarter of all UK adults, regularly visit their local waterway.

◄ *Plenty of evidence still exists of the canals' original use.*

conduits for the laying of a network of fibre-optic cables, whilst the canals themselves have been identified as a means to transfer water around the country as a form of 'national water grid'. More recently, the massive potential for waterside development has been reignited; it seems that even if you can't travel along the canals having a view of them has turned from being a positive disadvantage to something that adds considerably to the value of a property.

As modern life becomes more complex and time becomes something measured in nanoseconds, drifting along the canal network in a narrowboat offers a unique opportunity to reconnect with the past, enjoy the present and contemplate the future. Once the mainspring of the industrial revolution, the canals became increasingly marginalised to a point where their very existence was threatened. Rescued just in time, they have found a new role at the very heart of our national consciousness and seem destined to stay there for some time yet.

Did you know?
Two hundred new miles of canal have been added in the last decade, meaning the network is growing again for the first time since the mid-nineteenth century.

◁ *Dundas Aqueduct over the River Avon outside Bath.*

APPENDIX 1 – KEY CANAL TERMS

Aft	The back of a boat (also known as the stern)
Arm	Offshoot from a main waterway
Balance Beam	The protruding arm used to operate a lock gate
Beam	A boat's width
Bow	The front of a boat
British Waterways	Authority responsible for the canals
Butty	Narrowboat without an engine
Cassion	Metal box capable of holding a boat
Cill	Step inside a lock that the gates sit on
Cut	Alternative name for a canal
Draught	Depth of a boat
Fender	Detachable protection, usually made of rope, plastic or rubber
Flight	A series of consecutive locks

Galley	A boat's kitchen
Gongoozler	A person who watches boat activity
Guillotine Lock/Bridge	Where the lock gate or bridge rises
Helmsman	The person steering the boat
Legging	A means of moving a boat down a tunnel without using mechanical power
Lift Bridge	A bridge that needs to be winched up
Number 1	A boatman who owned his own boat
Paddles	Trapdoors in the side of a lock which the water passes through
Pound	The section of a canal between locks
Puddle	Clay mixture that forms a waterproof lining for canals
Rudder	The blade that steers a boat underwater
Staircase	Locks where the bottom gate of one is the top gate of the next

Stop Planks	Wood used to form a temporary barrier for water or boats
Summit	The highest portion of a canal
Swing Bridge	A bridge that swings out to let boats through
Tiller	The handle that steers the rudder
Turnover Bridge	A bridge constructed to allow a horse pulling a boat to switch sides of a canal
Wharf	Place where boats load or unload their cargoes
Winding	The process of turning a boat, so called because it originally involved harnessing the wind
Winding Hole	Place where a boat can be turned around
Windlass	The 'key' used to operate the winding gear on a lock

To learn more about the narrowboat story why not visit one of the following museums:

Boat Museum, Ellesmere Port
0151 355 5017
www.nwm.org.uk
Probably one of the most comprehensive waterways museums, spread out over seven acres with its own warehouse, locks and a particularly impressive display of old boats. Choose a good day as much of the collection is outdoors.

Canal Museum, Stock Bruerne
01604 862229
www.stokebruernecanalmuseum.org.uk
Stoke Bruerne is often described, quite reasonably, a typical example of a 'canal village', sandwiched between the southern portal of the Blisworth Tunnel and at the top of the Stoke Bruene flight of locks.

Foxton Canal Museum

0116 279 2657

www.fipt.org.uk

Home of the Foxton Inclined Plane Trust, dedicated to restoring this unique part of the waterways system, with the museum acting as a focal point for their activities in the lift's old boilerhouse.

Kennet and Avon Canal Centre, Devizes

01380 721279

www.katrust.org

Located in an old grain store and bonded warehouse, the centre (which also acts as the headquarters for the Kennet and Avon Trust) is sited just off the wharf at the top of the notorious Caen Hill flight in Devizes and focuses on the history of the Kennet and Avon Canal.

London Canal Museum

020 7713 0836

www.canalmuseum.org.uk

Housed in a Victorian ice house built for an ice-cream maker, this museum tells the story of London's canals. There's also a Bantam Tug, a working model of a lock and the opportunity to sit inside a reconstructed cabin and listen to a short radio play on how boating families lived.

Gloucester Waterways Museum

01452 318200

www.gloucesterwaterwaysmuseum.org.uk

Situated on the Gloucester Docks, this award-winning museum tells the story of the canals through video, photo and audio archives and has a collection of floating exhibits outside including the 1898 narrowboat *Northwich* and a steam dredger.

Yorkshire Waterways Museum, Goole
01405 768730
www.waterwaysmuseum.org.uk
Part of the Sobriety Project, this museum was developed to tell the story of the
Aire and Calder Navigation and the creation of the Port of Goole, and thereby
acknowledges the part that navigations played in the development of our waterways.

The following books offer a great insight into canals and boatmen:

Burton, Anthony & Pratt, Derek *The Anatomy of Canals: The Early Years* (The History
    Press, 2001)
Burton, Anthony & Pratt, Derek *The Anatomy of Canals: Mania Years* (The History
    Press, 2002)

Burton, Anthony & Pratt, Derek *The Anatomy of Canals: Decline and Renewal* (The History Press, 2003) – three books offering a comprehensive history of the canals

Corble, Nick *Britain's Canals: A Handbook* (The History Press 2007) – detailed but accessible guide to all things canal-related

Corble, Nick *James Brindley: The First Canal Builder* (The History Press, 2005) – biography of canal pioneer James Brindley

Corble, Nick *Walking on Water* (Belmont Press 2007) – fresh edition detailing a trip down the spine of the waterways system on the edge of the millennium

Hopkins, Tony & Brassley, Pat *Wildlife of Rivers and Canals* (Moreland Pub. Co., 1982) – guide to waterways wildlife

Rolt, L.T.C. *Narrow Boat* (Sutton Publishing, 1994) – revised edition of the book that started the revival of the canals

The following websites offer more information:

www.britishwaterways.co.uk – British Waterways
www.canalia.com – portal for canal-based holidays
www.canaljunction.com – aimed at hirers and owners but goes beyond these
www.canalmedia.co.uk – general resources
www.canals.com – comprehensive site on all things to do with canals
www.justcanals.com – claims to list most canal sites
www.waterscape.com – British Waterways leisure site

Art on sale.

Other titles available in this series

■ ISBN 978 0 7524 5605 8

■ ISBN 978 0 7524 5094 0

■ ISBN 978 0 7524 5914 1

■ ISBN 978 0 7524 5092 6

■ ISBN 978 0 7524 6452 7

■ ISBN 978 0 7524 6404 6